Copyright © 2017 , I Am A Natural Cutie
All Rights Reserved

Published by Favor House Publishing

Dedication:

To Harmony, your beautiful locs inspired me to write this story. Keep smiling pretty girl.

To Phoenix, my natural cutie, always keep going even when you feel like giving up. Love Tete!

To every cutie reading this story, know that you are beautiful naturally!

Phoenix woke up bright and early. Today is Monday but not just any 'ol Monday. Today is the first day of 'big' school!

Phoenix grabbed her comb, brush, and her favorite purple hair bows. She ran to her momma and asked, "Can you put the extra puffy-puffs in my hair? I'm a big girl now. Please, momma."

Her momma smiled and then gave Phoenix the prettiest, puffiest-puffs ever seen.

Phoenix hurried to finish getting ready because she did not want to be late on her first day.

She took one more look in the mirror and gave herself two thumbs up.

When they arrived at school, momma walked Phoenix to her new kindergarten class. She gave her a big kiss and told Phoenix, "Make it a great day, baby!"

Phoenix grabbed a seat at the big round table and waited to meet her new classmates.

Two girls came and sat at the table with her, but they did not talk to her.

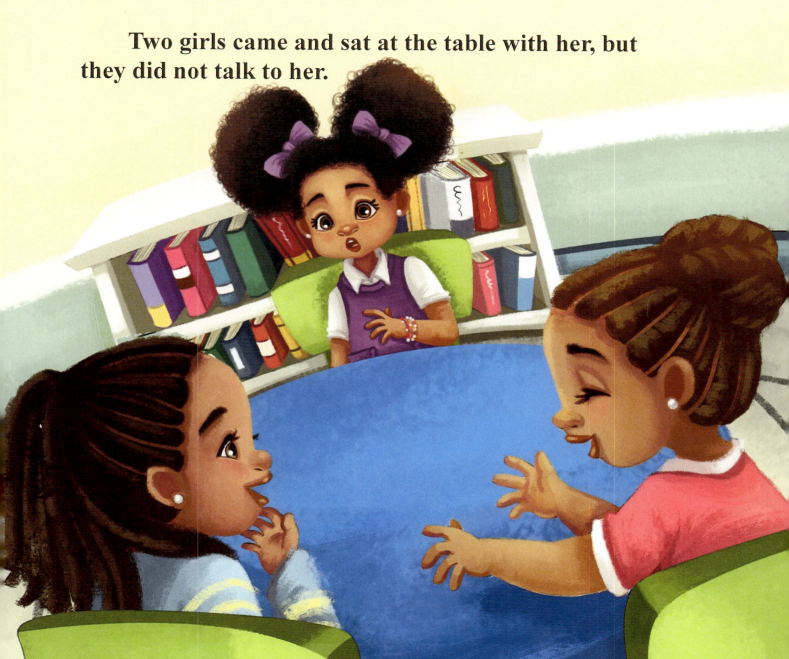

Phoenix smiled and waved at the girls. They smiled at each other, laughed, and then made fun of her extra puffy-puffs.

Phoenix became very sad and just wanted to go home to her momma.

She held her head down and told the teacher, Mrs. Melanin that she did not feel well. The teacher called Phoenix's momma, and she came back to the school right away.

Phoenix ran straight to momma and cried and cried. She told momma that she never ever wanted to go back to 'big' school because of what the mean girls did to her. Phoenix said that she didn't want to wear extra puffy-puffs ever again.

Momma was so surprised to hear all of this; she wrapped her arms around Phoenix and took her home for the day.

When they got home, momma sat Phoenix in front of the mirror and showed her that she had the same pretty puffs that she loved before she went to school.

Momma said, "Your hair is perfect just the way it is because it was created that way naturally. Your aunt, nana, and even your great-grandmother wore their hair just like yours."

"Really, momma? Wow!" said Phoenix.

"That's right," said momma. "There is so much power and strength in our hair. OUR hair grows out to reach the sun." momma said "We are natural cuties, baby!"

"But what if other people don't think it's so cute?" Phoenix asked

"Baby, everyone won't always like it or even uderstand the beauty and magic of your hair"

Phoenix wanted to know more about this magic.

Momma explained that her hair was sooooooo strong it could break even the toughest comb!

or sky the to up up, up,

"OUR hair has the power to stretch

down, down, down to the ground," said Momma

"Our hair could shrink into a small ball or it could puff out like a HUGE cloud!" momma continued.

Phoenix got so excited and became proud to have such special hair, just like the other women in her family! She jumped up and told momma, "I'm going back to school again because I'm a big girl! I'm a natural cutie."

The next day momma gave Phoenix two extra, extra puffy-puffs with two pretty purple bows. Momma walked Phoenix into the class. She told Phoenix, "Always remember how special you are and never forget the power in your hair."

Phoenix waved goodbye and ran to a seat at the same table with the two mean girls. They giggled and poked their tongues out as she took her seat. Phoenix just smiled and held her head high.

Ms. Melanin told the class to draw a picture of someone special. When they finished, everyone would share what they made with the rest of the class. Phoenix was excited because she loved to draw and she had the perfect idea for her picture

When the teacher asked who wanted to go first, Phoenix waved her hand and jumped out of her seat.

"I love that excitement, Phoenix!" said Mrs. Melanin. "You can go first." Phoenix came to the front of the room and proudly showed her picture to the class. One of the mean girls yelled out, "What is that?"

Phoenix smiled and proudly said, "This is a picture of my super hero family! We have power and strength in our extra puffy hair!"

The other mean girl asked, "Well where is your cape if you're a superhero?"

Phoenix laughed and said, "No silly, I don't need a cape!" with her head held high, she said "I'm a natural cutie, just naturally fly!"

The entire class loved her picture and Mrs. Melanin even let her hang it on the wall. When momma picked Phoenix up from school, she showed her the picture and said, "I taught them what it means to be a real, brave natural cutie."

Phoenix held her momma's hand and walked past the mean girls. They were still only able to see her puffy-puffs as a hairstyle, but Phoenix knew they were her superpower!

2016 Little Miss Natural Cutie Pageant.

Phoenix on her first day of kindergarten

Pam & Phoenix